HUW EVERY DAY CAN BE FRIDAY

The Secret to Superior Customer Service

MEYANA N. McCOMBS

Copyright © 2019

Meyana N. McCombs

ISBN (Book): 9781693780998

ISBN (Workbook): 9781693782947

Table of Contents

DEDICATION

First and foremost, I would like to thank God for blessing me with a gift that I love to share—the gift of in-
spiring and encouraging through my writing. I would
like to say thank you to all the people who purchased,
read, and shared the first edition of How Every Day
can be Friday—"The Secret to Meyana's Happiness."
Special thanks to my family whose support is out of
this world. I cannot thank you enough.

I would like to acknowledge my three kings in training—Kevonte, Lonnell, and Jamal. They support my
vision and share the mission. I could not do it without
your encouragement, support, and most importantly,
your love.

INTRODUCTION

A year after "How Every Day can be Friday: The Secret to Meyana's Happiness" was published, I realized that "The Secret to Meyana's Happiness" could become "The Secret to Superior Customer Service in the Workplace." Now, you must be thinking, is there really a secret to superior customer service and if so, why is it just now being revealed? I have been in the customer service industry since I was a teenager (I won't disclose how long that's been because then you would know my age). However, when I discovered that making people feel happy enhanced customer service, I decided it was time to write the second edition of "How Every Day can be Friday" *The Secret to Superior Customer Service.*

In the workplace, Friday is often the most popular day of the entire week. So "making every day Friday" was developed from my efforts to help ease my co-workers' continuous dread that Friday was "four days away from Monday." Not a good attitude for ideal customer service. I became so tired of them being unhappy and/ or having nothing to be happy about that I decided to bring Friday to them every day. I began working a job at an eye clinic on September 15, 2015, and by Thanksgiving 2015, I had the vision to make every day Friday. So, as you can see, it only took two months for me to realize that for our company to win, not only did we have to be on the same team, but we had to be on the same page. It took me exactly 90 days to convince myself that every day could be Friday, and once I was convinced, I decided to teach the world!

I have found in the past three years of promoting the maxim "every day is Friday" that it is not your fault or your workplace's fault why every day is not a good day. I blame it on social media, news media outlets, and anything that discredits the idea that every day can be great. It is detrimental to the success of your company if superior customer service is not a priority. Mondays should be happy, Tuesdays should involve teamwork, Wednesdays should be team building, Thursday should be about appreciation, and Fridays should be fun since they both begin with an "F." It's time to change the mindset and trajectory of your company by taking your customer service to a whole new level. In this book, you will find different principles, ideas, tips, and tools to level up your company's customer service Miss Friday's way!

CHAPTER 1
SMILING THROUGH THE RAIN

Experiencing "rain" on the job is something that is inevitable, and unfortunately, we all must go through. The good news is that you are not alone. I have experienced some rain throughout the years of my work history, so I can relate. Rain could be several different things—from mean bosses, unruly coworkers, small office space, random inspections, broken equipment, conflict amongst staff, staff shortage, sharing office with someone who smells bad, management changes every 90 days, not-so-friendly front desk staff, and/or being over worked and under paid, which may always and forever be the case for some. The list goes on, including:

- excessively high workloads with unrealistic deadlines that make people feel rushed, under pressure, and overwhelmed,

- a lack of control over work activities,

- a lack of interpersonal support,

- poor working relationships that lead to a sense of isolation,

- difficulty settling into a new promotion that you earned because of a lack of training,

- concerns about job security,

- lack of career advancement,

- bullying or harassment,

- micro-management,

- ineffective management, and/or

- failure to keep employees informed about significant changes to the business, causing uncertainty about the future and a loss of employee trust in the company.

You may have experienced some of this "rain." While you may exercise control over some of these experiences, others are simply out of your control. Often, workplace issues don't just pop up out the blue. They may have existed or developed over quite some time, but have never been resolved.

Every organization has a mission and every company has a team leader. I believe that behind every great leader are great employees. Every organization will be faced with different challenges, but it is the way that we smile through the trials as a team that makes all the difference. The wise man, Frederick Douglass, once said "If there is no struggle, there is no progress." So, while working on a job we must work as a team, fight through struggles as a team so that we can see progress and succeed as a team. Teamwork truly makes the team work. As organizations face different challenges, the way that their team works together will influence the success or failure of the company. In my workplace, I also figured that if we were going to work together for eight hours, we might as well treat each other like family.

In order to smile through the rain, we must first develop a mindset that every day can be Friday. Have you ever considered making every day a Friday? Seriously think about it for a second. Some people can attest to Mondays being miserable, Tuesdays are frustrating, Wednesday is worldwide Hump Day, Thursdays, people start becoming happy, and on Friday the world is expressing their own unique way of saying "TGIF"! I have found that most people who are stuck in this mentality don't necessarily hate the work they do, but they have been fed this negative way of thinking shared by many of the world's employees.

I have discovered that the happiness that is generated by making every day Friday sets me apart from anybody else in any other organization or company. I want you to feel the same happiness. What would possibly change for your company if management came to work feeling like every day was Friday? What about your employees? I used to work at a call center, and Mondays and Tuesdays were the worst. During these two days, we received the most calls. Wednesday was hump day and Thursday was the day before Friday—so, just like the rest of the business world, as the days got closer to Friday, I grew happier.

I saw my customer service job progress from 0-100 once I made every day Friday. The company didn't hire new employees. I didn't get a raise. And although management changed, it had nothing to do with that. My ultimate goal for making every day Friday was to promote positivity within the workplace. I wanted the result to be a family-oriented, team-driven, and mission-focused atmosphere within the workplace. Indeed, I literally saw lives change right in front of me simply because of the customer service that was provided.

Rain in the business forecast is not something new. The beauty of rain is that the sun comes out after a storm. Within the workplace, the sun's rays represent the solutions to problems. Rain, I believe, is a perfect opportunity for an organization to evaluate where they are and to strategize and put things on paper for their plan to execute. So, while you are thinking about the kinds of rain experiences you have faced in the workplace, jot down what you could do to help make the sun shine and improve your workplace.

CHAPTER 1
WRITING SESSION

Can you recall any "rain in the forecast" experiences you have faced in the workplace? How was it handled? Were you involved?

1.

_____

_____

_____

_____

_____

_____

2.

_____

_____

_____

_____

_____

_____

3.

_____

_____

_____

_____

_____

_____

_____

4.

_____

_____

_____

_____

_____

_____

CHAPTER 2
THE PROCESS

Would you agree that people often want results but are not willing to go through the process? Many life goals require you to go through a process—they start with the thought, the dream, the plan, and then the execution.

For example:

- building a business from scratch,

- writing a book and becoming a published author,

- developing your own clothing line and unique logo,

- opening up a restaurant, hair salon, barber shop, or your own nail salon, and becoming the top motivational speaker in the world.

With any of these efforts, you must go through a process. Taking your business' customer service to the next level will also require a process and a team effort.

Prior to the publication of my first book, "How Everyday can be Friday: The Secret to Meyana's Happiness,"

I didn't realize how much my perspective on the days of the week impacted my customer service. Now, although I thought my customer service was fairly decent, once my outlook changed, my customer service improved drastically. I had the chance to see people glow, lives changed, and excited faces when patients saw me at the front desk. It had reached the point where patients would not only request me to serve them, but if I wasn't there, they were disappointed. So it wasn't that my customer service was previously bad, but I was working without the connection of passion—it was working just for the paycheck. Once I acknowledged that my job could never pay me for my true worth, I accepted a new assignment to spread joy within the workspace. This became a priceless feeling.

Although it only took me 90 days to convince myself that every day could be Friday, I definitely went through a process. My goal was to make every day a good day no matter what day of the week it was. Instead of Mondays being miserable, Mondays became magical; instead of Tuesdays being frustrating, Tuesdays became good; instead of Wednesdays being the middle of the week, Wednesdays became Hump Day; instead of Thursday not being Friday, Thursdays became Friday Eve; and instead of Friday being just Friday it was "Thank God it's Friday"! Across the globe, people have held different opinions about the days of the week and many predict how the week will unfold depending on their perception, or the adjective they use to describe each week day. It is not until your mindset changes that you will be able to see and feel the difference. For example, took me 89 days to convince my co-worker—who initially didn't want every day to be Friday—that every day could be a good day. How much more effective would you work ethic or effort be if you were not solely focused on the day of the week? We must accept that we become a reflection of our attitudes.

In our daily decision making it is often easy to abort, avoid, or try to eliminate any process. One reason that people don't like to go through processes is because it requires more effort. So, it sounds good and even convincing to make every day Friday, but going through the actual process of changing mindsets is intimidating. I must be honest that prior to making every day Friday I was a little frightened of people believing in me and/or even agreeing with concept. So, for me, going through the process of mindset change was not easy. However, as I begin to see things change, lives transformed, and customer service levels rise, I knew I had no choice but to see it through to the end. Another word for avoiding any process is simply fear. The flip side of fear is victory. So, even though I was afraid, and at times, doubtful that every day could be Friday, once the process began and I began to see progress, it became easier.

At times, customer service is not the forefront of organizations, but becomes important once a complaint is addressed. In reality, customer service should not be optional—a focus on customer service ought to be as mandatory as the budget. Customer service is a continuous, daily process. It must not be overlooked, and should be stressed as an important factor during employee orientations. In my efforts to make every day Friday, I was trying to find a way to make the workplace more soothing and to make patients feel welcome. In 2018, I noticed the drastic change in customer service within our workplace. This enhanced customer service we experienced was the icing on the cake.

CHAPTER 2
WRITING SESSION

Can you recall one or more processes you have experienced to enhance the customer service of your company?

1.

_____

_____

_____

_____

2.

_____

_____

_____

_____

3.

_____

_____

_____

_____

4.

_____

_____

_____

_____

CHAPTER 3
THE POWER OF POSITIVITY

Positivity is a game changer in the workplace, today. When it comes to positivity, it is imperative that management is part of the solution, not part of the problem. Have you ever heard the saying "its starts from the top"? Often, because management is considered "higher up," it deceives them into thinking that what they do doesn't matter. Positivity matters. When companies and organizations don't understand the effect of manager's negativity on employees, they continuously hire new staff without fixing the attitude problem at the top. In contrast, every great leader has the potential to produce great employees through positivity.

I had no idea that positivity could do so much in the workplace. Check out my story:

On September 15th, 2015 I started working at an eye clinic. When I arrived, every day was not Friday. Every day was not happy. Every day had nothing to do with teamwork, productivity, or putting in a 120% effort. Every day had nothing to do with spreading love or providing the best customer service possible. In short, every day had nothing to do with an assignment to make the world a better place. I had adopted the world's negative mindset toward the work week. Then, I began to look at things differently from the outside in. So instead of being consumed with negativity, I begin to study the work day—my co-workers' and the doctor's moods, attitudes and postures. I continued to do that until November 24th, 2015.

The next step in my journey towards the power of positivity was the day I began to write. My positivity led to positive change within the workplace. I was happy to come to work every day, but something dropped in my spirit of making every day Friday. I noticed that the energy level, sweet aroma, and attitude in the workplace should have been recorded. I wished there had been a TV crew to record the positive changes that my workplace experienced.

I was not mad that my colleagues were not grateful for every day. I decided that teaching others how to make every day Friday would bring them the same flavor of positivity that it brought me, so that's what I did. I came up with the topics that I would write about to encourage other people not only to make every day Friday, but to make the best out of every day. The topics were as following: smiling through the rain, the process, having a different mindset, how everyday can be payday, trying something new, dealing with multiple attitudes, practice what you preach, and positive thinking quotes. It took me just 30 days to write my book, and by December 25th, 2015, I had a rough draft for my family to review and provide feedback.

Since I wasn't ready to publish the book yet, I decided to implement everything within the book at my workplace to see if the "every day can be Friday" concept really worked. After all, before you can convince anybody that what you have will work, you must be convinced yourself. It took me literally 90 days to convince myself that every day could be Friday. Once I was convinced, it raised my belief to a whole new level. It was that moment that I wanted to be sure to smile through the rain no matter what I was going through, and or currently facing in my life. I didn't want to abort the process and knew in order to convince others it would take hard work and dedication. I knew that I had to have a different mindset.

Every day can be payday was my way of gaining a deeper appreciation of seeing "another day" versus "another day coming and you not making it." I had to try something new by going against the grain no matter what came my way. In the workplace in general you will have to deal with multiple attitudes and there is nothing that you can do about it. Practice what you preach was my way of not just talking the talk, but walking the walk. And positive thinking quotes was the section where I wanted people to regain any hope that could have been lost that better days do really come.

So, the story gets even better. A year after writing and announcing that I was going to publish a book, I received an offer to leave my job. Now, I didn't really want to go, but at the time, it seemed like a better opportunity. The funny part about a better opportunity is that sometimes that better opportunity is right in front of you, but you may not actually see it. When I left, the concept and implementation of "making every Friday" ceased. Patients wanted to know what in the world happened to me. It turns out that I was hired at the new company for the wrong position. I was laid off from work, and ended up at home, unemployed. So thankfully, when my old position at the front desk became available again, my previous employer called me back to work. I returned to work at the clinic on April 16th, 2017. I got back in to the swing of things quickly—I felt like I was back home and back to myself.

Instead of complaints, we received compliments. We were often told that we had the best customer service in the entire hospital. Lives were transformed and the workplace began to feel like a home away from home—a place I look forward to coming to daily. My efforts weren't just for me, but to experience and witness the joy it brought to so many others. Instead of our front desk being toxic, not welcoming, and disorganized, I developed an atmosphere of positivity that was family oriented, team driven, and mission focused. I implemented the thought that if I had to work with you for 8 hours per day, we might as well treat each other like family.

At this point people had gotten tired of me talking about the book and kept asking well when is the book coming out? So, I was now faced with the challenge of finding a way to publish my work. I had begun to doubt where they money would come from and with the state of my bank account and hourly salary, I didn't think it was possible. However, it was not only the financial side that discouraged me. One publishing company had accepted my book concept, but required a word count of over 10,000 to qualify for publication. I only had 3,248 words, so needed to write at least 7,000 more. I was thinking how in the world that could be done. I didn't think it was possible. One day I was encouraged by another author who recommended I could just add more chapters to the book. I took the advice and wrote in excess of 12,000 additional words.

So now I had the word count, but I still was wondering about whether I had the funds. The publishing company was too expensive, so I decided to not go with them. A few weeks later—on a Friday—I decided to hire someone to help me move forward with the self-publishing process. It was not expensive and the book was released two Fridays later, on Friday, September 8th, 2017. I am now a successfully published author. No fancy degree. No filthy rich parents. I was a young lady with a vision and a plan to promote positivity within the work place. The moral of the story is that positivity makes a huge impact within the workplace and beyond.

CHAPTER 3
WRITING SESSION

Can you write down how the power of positivity has affected your life? Would you say that you are an overall positive person?

_____

_____

_____

_____

_____

_____

_____

_____

_____

_____

_____

CHAPTER 4
PAYDAY

Paydays often remind me of Fridays because no matter the amount of the check and/or whether most the check must be spent on bills, people are usually still happy. You may recall the Johnny Kemp song, "Just Got Paid (It's Friday Night)." So, if you get paid AND its Friday, then it indeed brings about a TGIF kind of attitude. However, I would like for you to extend your thinking, stretch your mindset and expand your horizon by imaging that every day you wake up is payday. Adopting the mindset of how every day can be payday is what I like to call next level thinking. In essence, whether physically or emotionally, you are paying or being paid, daily—you are the giver or the receiver. Your payday can be translated physically by you just waking up the next day. Your payday can be expressed naturally—when someone randomly treats you to lunch, or when you are a blessing to someone else and treat them to lunch. Your payday can be emotional, by being grateful for having enough food to eat. Last but not least, your payday can be as simple as being quietly focused in your right mind—being able to think clearly and for yourself.

Every day we pay or are paid in some form or fashion. However it is up to you to acknowledge the daily compensations that we often take for granted. It is funny that we are deceived into thinking that money can buy happiness and love. But it really can't. Some people, regardless if they admit or acknowledge it, will try to buy friendships. This is impossible. Simply because you have a lot of money doesn't mean that you will be happy all the time, so if I were you I wouldn't just choose money. People often try to buy love, but the truth is that love is free—whether you are giving or receiving it. I came to the realization that every day would be payday for me if I could become content with what I already have, what I am given, and simply seize the every opportunity, at every moment, 24 hours a day.

Within the workplace, employees tend to compare one's work ethic, pay scale, and/or misinterpret one's talent. There is a saying "you can never be paid for what your worth." I used to agree with this concept until I discovered that you are paid according to the amount of effort that goes into your daily routine. See, what separated me from everyone else on my job was that I was willing to go the extra mile, willing to sacrifice staying late if needed, and willing to give 120% effort even when I didn't feel like it. I believe a lot of people get looked over or not considered for promotion based on how they value themselves. What I mean by that is simply whether your making $60,000 or $100,000 a year, you must value yourself by what you're displaying versus what is required to be displayed. No matter how much money you have, what you are paid, or your retirement pension, being paid every day starts from within. You can do one of two things when you are told what to do on a regular 9 to 5 job. You can discover other ways to develop revenue with your gifts and talents and/or you can be complacent and stay where you are because it's convenient.

Whether it be physically, naturally, or emotionally, being paid every day is not for someone else to decide. It is up to you. By taking care of yourself physically, the benefits will pay off later in life. Being emotionally healthier is a great way to start to enjoy every day being payday on your terms. When you have a better understanding of your assignment to make the world a better place, being paid every day will come naturally. This is an asset for enhancing customer service in the workplace. See what employees may not know is that they are not just coming to work because they are on the schedule or payroll, but they are just as important as the owners, the founders, and the upper management. Employees just want to know that they belong and that their belonging has nothing to do with their salary or job title.

CHAPTER 4
WRITING SESSION

Can you name a time where you felt like you didn't matter on a job? What made you feel that way? If you were in the management position, how would you have handled it differently?

_____

_____

_____

_____

_____

_____

_____

_____

_____

CHAPTER 5
EXECUTION

Execution is carrying out or putting into effect a plan, order, laws, mission statement, company policy, or general rule. Execution as it pertains to the workplace is often not as easy as it sounds. Sometimes, despite new employee orientation, new hire training, and/ or employee handbooks, these rules seem to only be implemented in the beginning.

A plan is the first step to reaching a goal. But, for the plan to be fulfilled, you must execute. There is no way around making anything happen if execution is not a part of the recipe. If laws and orders are given, yet the recipient does not cooperate and the laws and orders are not adhered to, how can the goals be fulfilled? Mission statements tend to be my favorite simply because a mission statement reflects the organization's essence. The mission statement is what is used to convince a potential buyer, a partner, or even used as an elevator speech to promote business.

Execution in the workplace matters. When company management is aware that their customer service team needs some help, it is management's job to implement a refresher course for the staff. For example, there was a lady who complained to Walmart management about an employee who was unruly, impatient, and totally un-professional. If Walmart receives complaints about the same person for 30 days straight but fails to implement change by neglecting to address the issue, they will run into a customer service defect. They could end up losing customers, revenue, and eventually employees.

Execution is a team effort, so if we show up as a team and play as a team, then we will succeed as team! I like to call this the "Team Golden Rule" for any organization.

Let's execute from the beginning. This way, we won't have to revisit refresher courses because we will always be ready. Using execution to enhance a company's customer service is like updating software and convert-ing over to Windows 10 from Windows 97. It doesn't mean that the software is unusable, it just means that as technology progresses, you should also progress. Poor customer service in the workplace is detrimental to growth, expansion, and the livelihood of the organiza-tion. However, a company with exceptional customer service may very well attract customers and lead to increase growth and improved organizational success.

Have you ever stopped yourself from being rude or disrespectful to a waitress because you thought about how it would feel if someone treated you that way? Customer services requires empathy. You must imagine yourself in the customer's place. I believe that companies must train employees to be understand-ing and responsive in order provide well-executed customer service.

Even though top management may feel like they have it all together, evidence proves that if management lacks customer service skills, integrity, good character, or professionalism, the apple normally doesn't fall far from the tree. Execution is not a one-way street. As in any relationship whether part-owners or business partners, it is a team effort. Managers, owners, supervisors, and potential leaders must set the standards of executing action for the team's efforts.

Execution of the mission statement is what success is to your business plan.

—Miss Friday

CHAPTER 5
WRITING SESSION

Can you come up with different execution plans to improve your company?

_____

_____

_____

_____

_____

Communication Execution Plan

_____

_____

_____

_____

_____

Mission Statement Execution Plan

_____

_____

_____

_____

_____

Team Step Execution Plan

_____

_____

_____

_____

_____

Execution Action Plan

_____

_____

_____

_____

_____

CHAPTER 6
DISCIPLINE AND DEALING WITH MULTIPLE ATTITUDES

There are all kinds of people in the world today. We all have different lifestyles, cars, families, careers, educational backgrounds, and typically, different mindsets and multiple attitudes. I believe there are four specific areas that need to be perfected in order for a customer service professional to be equipped to deal with multiple attitudes.

People fall into one of four categories:

1. those who lack discipline,

2. those who don't understand the power of words and a smile. Kind words and a smile are contagious and could very well make someone's day.

3. those who must learn to love each other, accept people for who they are, and be kind and loving to all people.

4. those who must know the difference between being offensive and being objective. These people must learn to deescalate situation with positivity.

Of these four, I find that lack of discipline requires the most explanation, I will focus on this category.

There is nothing wrong with lacking discipline in certain areas. However, the problem begins when you are not able to admit you lack discipline. I find people lack the most workplace discipline in a few specific areas—time management, integrity and character within leadership, inconsistent rules, and lack of team effort.

Time Management

Time management is the ability to use your time wisely within the eight hours you're given to complete an assignment or task. Now, although time cannot be managed literally, you can manage your life events in relation to time. As it pertains to things such as managing your hours at work and managing your time generally—after work, for self-care, for studying, and for family. You often hear people say that there is just not enough time in a day to get everything done. You also hear people say that they need more money, more credit and even a third or fourth job when really, they just need to stop living beyond their means. Money and time are both valuable and limited. It is imperative that time is protected like your life depended on it, as it does. Use time wisely like your job is on the line, and budget it as if you will lose everything if you didn't. I like to think that it has a lot to do with just managing the time that we have and dispensing it properly. Poor management results in non-effectiveness and proper management results in effectiveness, efficiency, and great results. You literally are given 24 hours in a day which is 1,440 minutes or 86,400 seconds a day to get the job done!

Unfortunately, there is usually one person in the workplace who comes late every day, never turns in projects on time, and has difficulty following simple instructions. To avoid being this person, take control of your time management. Being able to properly manage your time is a skill that will be useful throughout your career and business if you master it early. To evaluate your time management skills, ask yourself these questions:

- who is in charge of how I spend my time?

- do I have any priorities in place?

- what tools am I using to keep track of time?

- am I organized or all over the place?

- have I sought wise counsel regarding time management?

- how much do I procrastinate?

- have I completed a self-evaluation of my time wasters?

- is it wise for me to multi-task?

- do I find myself putting everybody on my schedule but me?

Integrity and Character within Leadership

Some people think that you can be born with integrity and a good character. I have reason to believe that we are only born with a personality and the rest will come with experience. Leaders who have the strength of character and integrity often value three things: 1) honesty, 2) commitment and 3) trustworthiness.

Through their leadership, they inspire trust and loyalty in those whom they lead. Leaders tend to make decisions based on personal conviction and not necessarily due to popular opinion. Because of their integrity, good leaders don't do what is right because it's easy, convenient, or personally beneficial. They do it because it's right. Leaders are firm in their decision making, consistent with sticking to protocol, and know how to work well under pressure. There is nothing better than a leader with integrity, character, and a little humor— especially when tense situations need to be diffused.

There is a saying "There are too many chiefs and not enough Indians." I just think that it basically means there are a lot of people who say they want the leadership role and would like to take charge, yet not enough performance to align with the request. Although there is initially one leader put in charge, there are other leaders who are being trained to lead in the future. Leading with character and integrity breed things such as a family-oriented, team-driven, and a mission-focused atmosphere that assures success.

When you are looking for a job or working toward a promotion, the qualities of education and seniority may be negotiable—character, integrity, and work ethic are non-negotiable.

When I was the receptionist at the front desk of the eye clinic, I wasn't just your typical front desk clerk. I didn't talk the same, greet the same, smile the same, or answer the phone the same. I was like nothing that the world had seen before. I had implemented making every day Friday. I expressed love and provided the best customer service possible. When patients would come into the Ophthalmology Department, they felt welcomed. They often told me that I needed to be cloned! When the office called me back after my first book was published my book, I was awarded a promotion to the position I hold now as a Resident Coordinator. It one thing when you apply for a job because the position is open, but it is quite another to be recommended for a position because of your character and integrity. Although I wasn't technically qualified for the job, I was up for the challenge, and management had faith in my character, integrity, and work ethic.

"People will forget what you said, people will forget what you did, but people will never forget how you made them feel," says author and poet Maya Angelou.

Consistency with Rules

As a leader, it is not always easy to set the rules, but your character and integrity must be reflected in these rules. Rules are put in place not to control anyone but to keep order on the job.

There are all kinds of people when it comes to enforcing, setting, and obeying rules within the workplace. There will always be a group of folks who don't like rules but follow them, then you have the ones who don't follow the rules period, and then there are the "by the book" employees. The key to keeping order in the workplace is to be consistent with the rules that are set in place for the organization to run smoothly.

Employees who don't like rules but follow them are likely those who know the importance of having a job so they just want to keep the peace. The employees who don't follow any of the rules are the ones whose ego and pride are in the way—if things ever hit the fan, they would be the first to go. Lastly, you have the "by the book" employees who are typically the ones that the boss can rely on to keep things in order when they are out. They are normally the ones who get promoted because of their work ethic.

For the employees who don't understand why rules are put in place, I will name a few.

- rules help employees understand the company's expectations

- rules allow decision making without repeatedly interrupting management

- rules commend a person good work ethic and allows for equal opportunity

- rules keep the lines of communication open

- rules provide a healthy and stable workplace environment for both the employer and the employee

lack of Team Effort

I am a convinced that teamwork within the job makes the dream work. It is funny to me that teamwork doesn't usually just start after you begin professional work—It begins within school, work, relationships, home, marriage, partnerships and parenting. Whether in sports, school systems, the military, the medical field, or in colleges and organizations, having a strong team allows individual talents to stand together during good times and can keep the team moving forward during the difficult times.

Every organizational workplace has a team and a mission statement that they seek to fulfill daily. The mission statement generally includes the company goals (what they plan to do), and the rules, strategies and assignments for how they plan to accomplish this goal. A CEO, President, or management team cannot operate alone and the mission statement helps leadership guide employees in understanding the organization. The purpose of teamwork within the organization is to successfully ensure that the everyone's gifts and talents are properly applies to accomplish the mission to the best of the company's ability. It is important that the employer makes the employee or potential employee fully aware that they matter and that without their role the mission cannot be accomplished. Everybody simply wants to know that what they do matters and that is why is it good to know your gift, accept your gift, master your gift, and then perfect it to the best of your ability. It is important to value yourself and value your team.

CHAPTER 6
WRITING SESSION

Time Management Affirmation

Integrity and Character Affirmation

Consistency with Rules Affirmation

_____

_____

_____

_____

_____

Teamwork Affirmation

_____

_____

_____

_____

_____

CHAPTER 7
EMPLOYEES TODAY, LEADERS TOMORROW

I firmly believe that the maxim "employees today, leaders tomorrow," as it pertains to having great leadership within your organization. However, this doesn't only apply to the workplace. Think about it for a second. When we are in school and the leaders try to quiet the students during instruction time yet you have some students who do not listen. What happens is that the students who are not paying attention miss their turn to be the leader for the day. A teacher's job is to develop the leaders for tomorrow. However, if the students are not executing the plan that was set before them, how can their mission be accomplished? This also pertains to the workplace. We may start off as newly hired employees, but as we progress, it is up to us to become the leader that we were born to be.

I found that instilling excellent customer service qualities within an employee today will lead to a five-star, superior customer service leader, tomorrow. Would you agree that behind every great leader is a great employee? Before you can lead, you must learn to follow. Employees today and leaders tomorrow is a concept I believe every organization should implement. As a leader you must recognize your position of authority and maximize every moment to train your subordinates to be better than you. Companies should always offer advancement courses, additional training, and growth opportunities. As more leaders are developed, more of the world can be reached, and more things can be accomplished.

Superior customer service professionals are made up of employees who have been charged to give it their all and to make every day at work the best day, no matter what. I believe that prior to hiring and/or at monthly meetings, employees should complete a survey of what a kind leader they are and/or how far they want to go with the company. This will give current leadership a better understanding of who is up for the next level training.

Superior customer service is revealed as a person who is grateful and passionate about the position they hold within their company. In other words, they apply "The Golden Rule of Execution" which is: "show up as a team, play as a team, and you will succeed as a team!" There is nothing better for management than to know they can count on their employees. That's why management must dig a little deeper during the interview process to make sure every potential employee has at least the main three things characteristics of a what I call a great leader: 1) a learner, 2) a listener, and 3) a team player.

CHAPTER 7
WRITING SESSION

What positive impact would you expect if the hiring managers developed the concept of "employees today, leaders tomorrow," and acted accordingly?

If you are in any form of management, what are your thoughts? And lastly if you are an employee, do you feel like you are treated as a potential leader for the company?

_____

_____

_____

_____

_____

_____

_____

_____

_____

_____

CHAPTER 8
MISS FRIDAY'S POSITIVE AFFIRMATIONS

The process of first changing our mindset and our perspective in making every day a good day is the secret
to superior customer service within the workplace.

—Miss Friday

Positive thinking is free of charge! I challenge you to
start thinking positively daily and watch the outcome!

—Miss Friday

You were born to be a leader in your own way!

—Miss Friday

Not understanding your role within the organization is
detrimental to you acknowledging, accepting,
owning, and perfecting your position!

—Miss Friday

The AAOP Model to securing your identity is to:
Acknowledge, Accept, Own, and
Perfect the one in the mirror!

—Miss Friday

MONDAY THROUGH FRIDAY AFFIRMATIONS

MARVELOUS MONDAY AFFIRMATION

Today will be a great day.
Today I will act my best,
think my best, and give my best.
Today I realize that what I do matters
and that kindness go both ways.
Today I am determined to make
this a Marvelous Monday.

MONDAY THROUGH FRIDAY AFFIRMATIONS

THANKFUL TUESDAY AFFIRMATION

Today will be amazing.
Today, I give 120 % effort because
I owe it to myself.
Today I will think before I speak,
pause before I respond,
and not respond emotionally.
Today I will take the lead in being
thankful on this Tuesday
that will never be seen again.

MONDAY THROUGH FRIDAY AFFIRMATIONS

WINNING WEDNESDAY AFFIRMATION

Today will be a winning day.
Today I plan to win.
I will show up to win, I will play to win,
and I won't stop until I win.
Today I am convinced that everything
attached to me wins, and because of that,
today will be a Winning Wednesday.

MONDAY THROUGH FRIDAY AFFIRMATIONS

TRIUMPH THURSDAY AFFIRMATION

Today will be like never before.
Today I will achieve triumph on my job,
within my school day, and in my business.
I will smile through my trials and tribulations.
Today I will not allow my situation to change
my praise, but my praise to shift my situation.
Today will be Triumph Thursday
because I am claiming it.

MONDAY THROUGH FRIDAY AFFIRMATIONS

FANTASTIC FRIDAY

Today will be a Fantastic Friday
because I am in it.
Today I will forget about those days
left behind me and focus more on
fulfilling my duties for today.
Today I will execute positively by speaking
only good things from my lips
and displaying good actions.
Today will be a Fantastic Friday for me
and for you.

CHAPTER 8
WRITING SESSION

Create your own weekend affirmations for Saturday and Sunday.

Saturday

_____

_____

_____

_____

_____

_____

_____

_____

_____

_____

Sunday

_____

_____

_____

_____

_____

_____

_____

_____

_____

_____

ABOUT THE AUTHOR

Meyana "Miss Friday" McCombs is a proud Author of two books (1) "How Everyday Can Be Friday-The Secret to Meyana's Happiness" and (2) "Know Your Worth." She is young, vibrant, a sought-after writer, encourager, and overall atmosphere shifter. She is passionate about customer service in the workplace and is always looking for ways to improve her personal customer service skills.

"How Every Day can be Friday: The Secret to Superior Customer Service" originated from Miss Friday's first edition of "How Everyday can be Friday." Her first book was proven to not only improve customer service in the workplace but helped many people change their perspective to everyday life. Through her writing and sharing of stories, she hopes that the reader will gain some knowledge, ideas, tips, and tools as it pertains to taking your company's customer service to the next level.

Miss Friday wants companies to have hope that all is not lost, and for them to understand that customer service is the key to a successful business.

Made in the USA
Middletown, DE
01 January 2023

17836365R00033